freedom

Spiritual Insights from the Great Traditions

To Malachite, Let no one & no thing

It is a notable feature of human life that in all cultures and in almost every part of the globe there have been men and women who have understood – as though from 'inside' – the origin and existence of things. The rest of us often call these clear-sighted people 'wise', and what they understand 'insights'.

Whatever time and circumstances such people are born into, what they ver limit you, With love Mum Nov. '03

say or write carries a common stamp, a natural authority and ease. Their statements sound true. The manner of their speech and the colour of their language and expression often vary greatly but what they say has a common character.

Perhaps by quietly contemplating these statements we can share something of their wisdom.

Avoid anything which

requires an excuse

MUHAMMAD

The mature person accepts his situation

and doesn't desire anything outside it

TZUÍSSU

The more we have

the less we own

MEISTER ECKHART

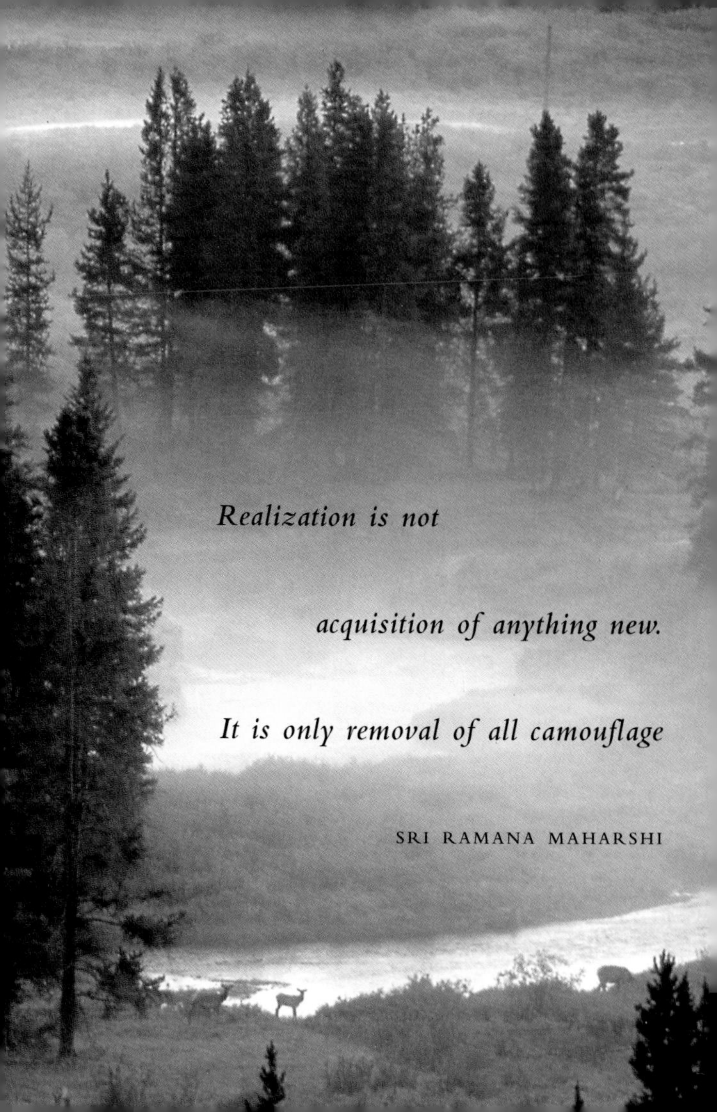
Realization is not
acquisition of anything new.
It is only removal of all camouflage
SRI RAMANA MAHARSHI

Who looks out with my eyes?

What is the soul?

I cannot stop asking.

If I could taste one sip

of an answer,

I could break out

of this prison for drunks

RUMI

Who cares about wealth and honour

Even the poorest thing shines

LAYMAN P'AN

The truth shall

make you free

JESUS

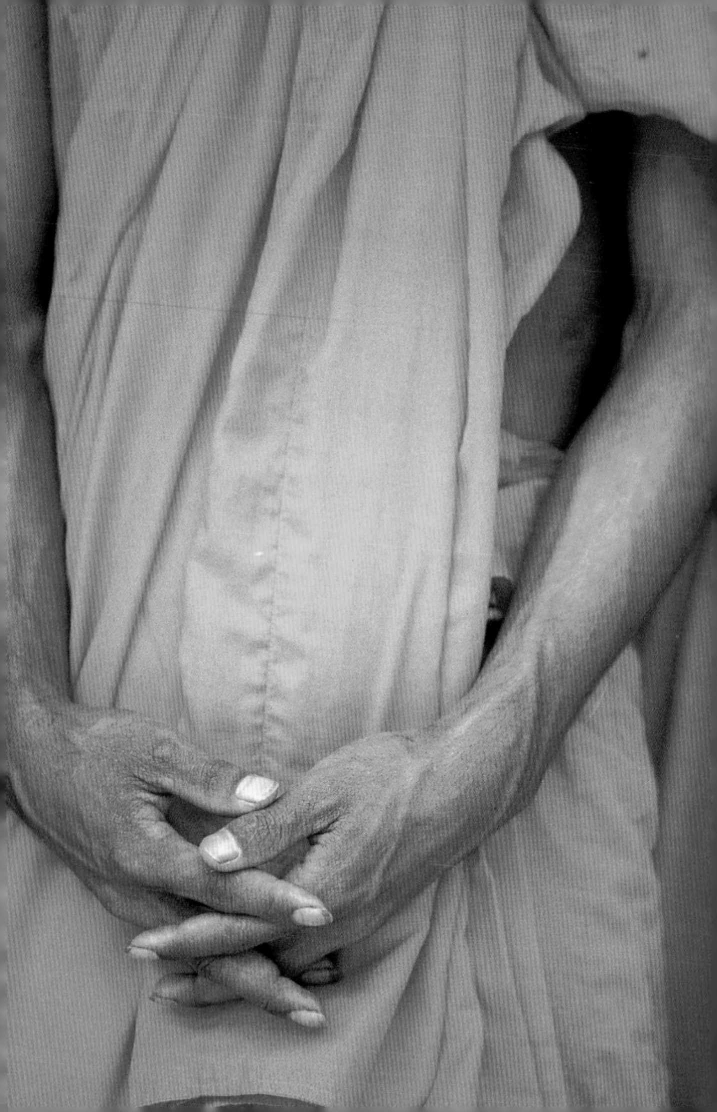

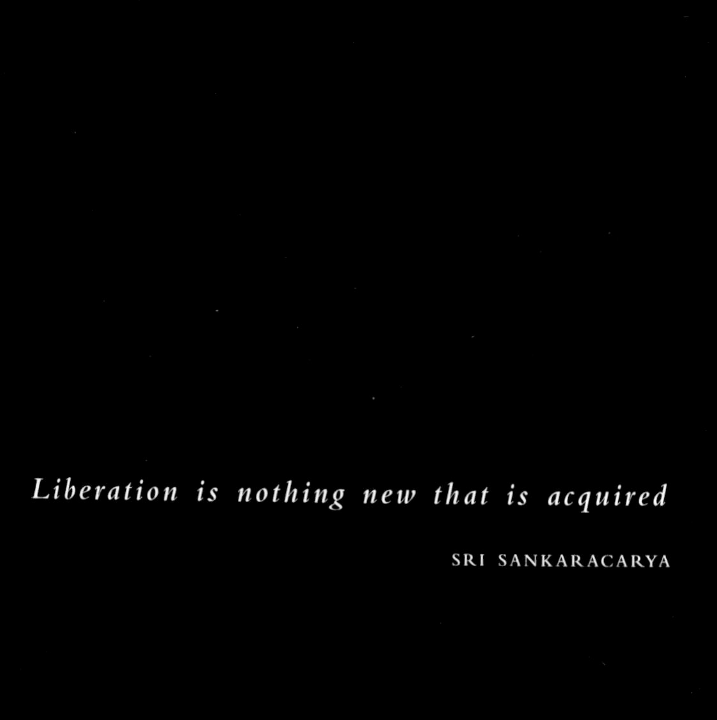
Liberation is nothing new that is acquired
SRI SANKARACARYA

There is no here, no there;

Infinity is right before your eyes

SENG TS'AN

In order to arrive at possessing

everything,

Desire to possess nothing

ST JOHN OF THE CROSS

The centre of the soul

is so infinite

that nothing can satisfy it

or give it any rest

but the infinity of

God

WILLIAM LAW

All know that the drop merges into the ocean

but few know that the ocean merges into the drop

KABIR

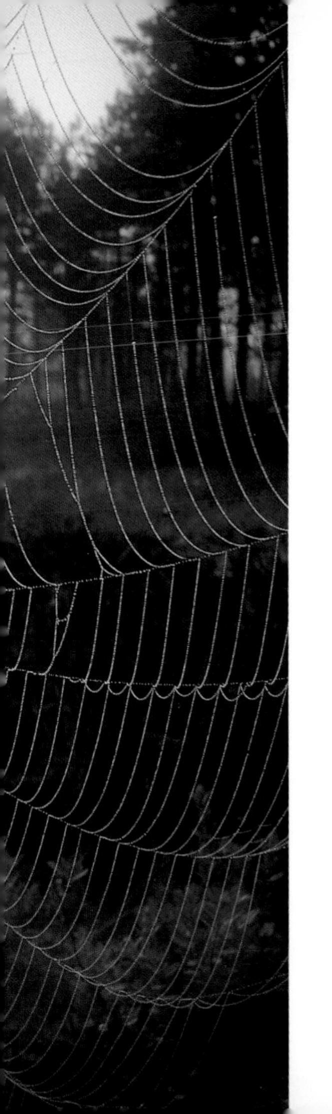

The silkworm

weaves its cocoon

and stays inside,

therefore it is imprisoned;

the spider weaves its web

and stays outside,

therefore it is free

CHINESE PROVERB

Where the Spirit of the Lord is, there is liberty

ST PAUL

Love the little trade which thou hast learned

and be content therewith

MARCUS AURELIUS

He I call liberated
who has trained his
mind to be still

DHAMMAPADA

If men thought of God as much

who would not attain liberation?

as they think of the world,

MAITRI UPANISHAD

You ask why I make my home

in the mountain forest,

and I smile, and am silent,

and even my soul remains quiet:

it lives in the other world

which no one owns

LI PO

The Great Way isn't difficult

for those who are unattached to their preferences.

Let go of longing and aversion,

and everything will be perfectly clear

SENG TS'AN

If you can walk on water

You are no better than a straw.

If you can fly in the air

You are no better than a fly.

Conquer thy heart

That you may become somebody

ANSARI

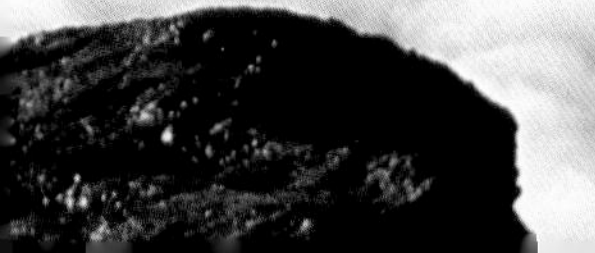

It is only in
accepting silence
that man can
come to know
his own spirit,
and only in
abandonment
to an infinite
depth of silence
that he can be
revealed to the
source of
his spirit

JOHN MAIN

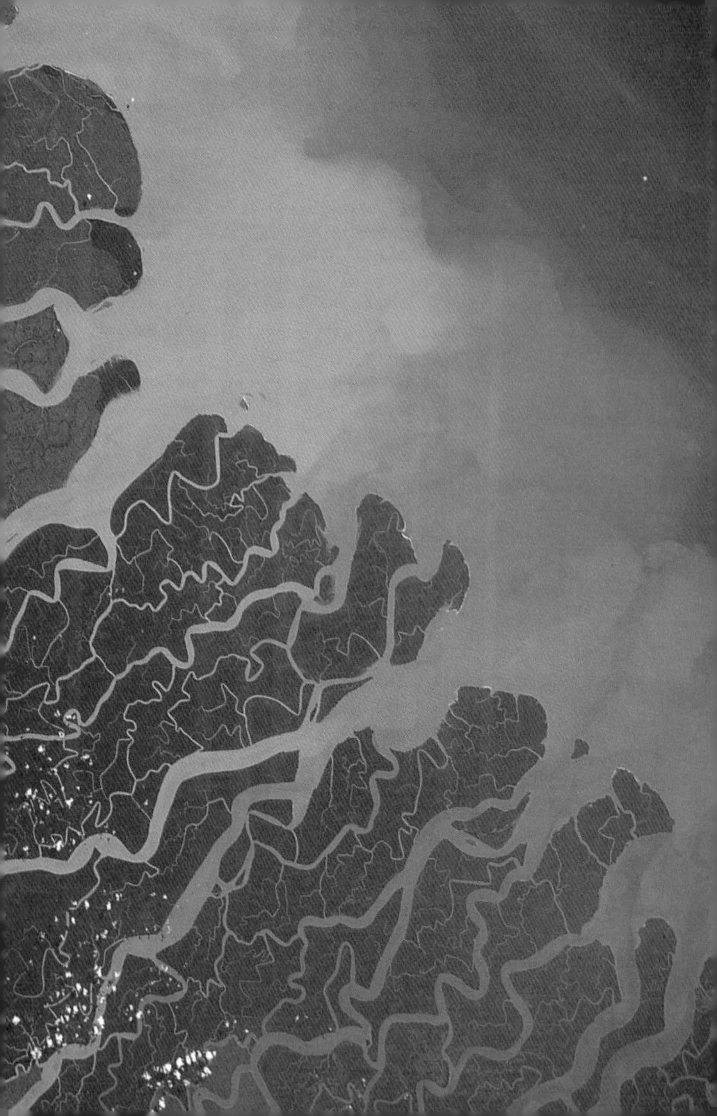

As rivers flowing into the ocean find their

final peace and their name and form disappear,

even so the wise become free from name

and form and enter into the radiance of the

Supreme Spirit

MUNDAKA UPANISHAD

Rise above all the pairs of opposing sensations;

and centred in the Self

be steady in truth, free from worldly anxieties,

BHAGAVAD GITA

We are not

We are not

troubled by

troubled by

things,

things,

but by the

but by the

opinions we have of

opinions we have of

things

things

EPICTETUS

The best knowledge is that which enables one to put an end to birth and death and to attain freedom from the world

BUDDHA

Give your life

to the one who

already owns

your breath and

your moments

RUMI

If you want to realise

the truth,

don't be for or against

SENG TS'AN

Try something different.

Surrender

RUMI

freedom

Published in England by

16 Orchard Rise, Kingston upon Thames, Surrey, KT2 7EY

Designed in association with
THE BRIDGEWATER BOOK COMPANY

Printed in Singapore

Editorial consultant: Philip Novak

The publishers would like to thank the Gettyone Stone Picture Library and The Image Bank for the use of pictures

ISBN 1 85645 552 1